APRIL DE ANGELIS

A Warwickshire
Testimony

faber and faber

First published in 1999
by Faber and Faber Limited
3 Queen Square, London WC1N 3AU

Typeset by Country Setting, Kingsdown, Kent CT14 8ES
Printed in England by Mackays of Chatham plc, Chatham, Kent

A CIP record for this book
is available from the British Library

ISBN 0-571-20355-8

2 4 6 8 10 9 7 5 3 1

A Warwickshire Testimony

April De Angelis' plays include *Positive Hour* (Out of Joint) *Playhouse Creatures* (Sphinx Theatre Company), *Hush* (Royal Court), *Soft Vengeance*, *The Life and Times of Fanny Hill* (adapted from the John Cleland novel) and *Ironmistress*. Her work for radio includes *The Outlander* (Radio 5), which won the Writers' Guild Award (1992), and, for opera, *Flight* with composer Jonathan Dove (Glyndebourne, 1998).

by the same author

plays
THE POSITIVE HOUR
PLAYS ONE
(*Ironmistress, Hush,
Playhouse Creatures, The Positive Hour*)

Introduction

The inspiration for this project came in the form of some material I was given in my own village of Clifford Chambers in Warwickshire. In 1970 a local interviewed the occupants of every house about their lives and their memories of the village. The stories were then published as part of a parish newsletter. Reading the stories, with their tantalising glimpses of quiet tragedies, acts of kindness, cruelty and endurance, seen from the 1970s and overlayed by my own 1990s perspective, convinced me that there was material here for a play.

The Royal Shakespeare Company then commissioned me to research material for the play and the project proper began when I invited the members of local communities around Stratford to contribute their own memories and impressions. From the resultant interviews and written material from groups and individuals, the 'testimony' was transcribed. The playwright, April De Angelis, was then asked to consider the material as the basis for a new play.

April's commission and my research were made possible by projects funding at The Other Place. This resource exists both to develop the skills of the RSC's creative artists and, among many other things, new writing projects.

A Shakespearean sense of the mundane sitting beside the momentous is apparent in many of the stories:

George was always proud of his work for he put all his heart into it. When he eventually had to give up gravedigging, he watched contractors hired by the undertakers. 'Untidy lot, ragged grave, soil just dropped anywhere, mess afterwards.' When little William died George returned from retirement one

last time and dug the grave. It was one of the
neatest jobs and after the funeral George beautifully
turfed over the grave. (Clifford Notes)

There were numerous references to death and the rituals
surrounding it. Many people mentioned the pig killings,
which everyone came to watch, celebrate and partake in.

Most people in our village had a pig in the sty.
They kept saddleback pigs. They relied on the pigs.
If you were a cottager and you had one or two pigs
you'd enter them in the pig club and a committee
man would come round to the cottage and look to
see that it was healthy and he'd write it into the
book. If anything happened to that pig, it was an
insurance, they paid out.

There was a fellow who lived by us and I used
to love to go with him on a Sunday morning. He'd
walk all round the pigsties to check on the pigs.
He was the pigkiller, the busiest man in winter, just
before Christmas. There was no fridges or freezers
or anything like that. Everybody lived magnificently
for a fortnight. It was all the spare ribs and the
pieces. They used to kill a pig November when the
frosts come in, when they were safe to do it. They'd
probably kill another one in March. I saw big pigs
pulled up into a plum tree, let the air get at it, and
it would hang there for a day and a night. Then a
man would come next day and cut it up for chops,
ham, sides of bacon. (Interview)

A generation which has experienced two world wars is
understandably preoccupied with violent death and
maiming:

I was hiding under the table. I daren't cough or
hardly breathe. My aunt said to my mother,
'Harriet, I hear the trunks are coming to the station

tomorrow at twelve o'clock.' This puzzled me.
I knew I must find out what the trunks were,
I could only think of trees. The next day, I ran all
the way down the Coventry Road to the station,
and went on the platform. There were lots of
people there. 'Here they come, here they come!' I
heard people say. The train pulled up. The station
porters were running rowards the train with
trolleys. I understood the words 'the trunks are
coming'. These poor soldiers, some had only their
trunk, no arms, no legs. I trembled all the way to
school. I daren't say a word to anyone, not to my
Mum or to anyone at school, because I wasn't
supposed to be there. (Interview)

From the testimonials comes a feeling that, despite the
appalling poverty and the 'feudal' relationship with the
'big house', there was a sense that a spiritual richness in
the community has now been lost:

Mrs Betteridge wore clogs (and she was one of the
last to wear the white bonnet so common years
earlier) and the echo of her clogs on the stone floor
could be heard the moment you knocked at her
front door. She kept poultry (which she killed and
dressed herself), ducks and pigs.
    Mr Betteridge was a bellringer and every New
Year's Eve after ringing in the New Year, he would
invite the other four bellringers back to his home
for a good supper of rabbit pie, cooked specially
for the bellringers by Mrs Betteridge. (Clifford
Notes)

There was one day in the life of our village seventy
years ago when the children were very much
involved with the grown-ups. That was May Day.
Miss Wilding practised them in the May singing.

Mrs Charlie Sylvester made the maypole out of two hoops decorated with flowers that the children had picked the evening before. Then, accompanied by the May Queen, the girls in their best dresses and laden with flowers and the boys in their stiff collars went round to each house singing May songs outside each door. The money collected went on the tea. Mrs Sylvester had a large garden at the back. Trestle tables were laid out and the children sat down to a scrumptious tea. (Clifford Notes)

Seventy years ago, The Hollies was a hive of activity. It was all carpenters, decorators, wheelwrights, undertakers, dairy, pig and poultry keepers, bee keepers and plum and apple growers. (Clifford Notes)

Ordinary people are being forced out of the village by high prices. Commuters are taking over from working class families and I do feel resentful about it. I'd give my eye teeth to go back there but I'll never be able to. The village is full of strangers, the old families gone away. The pub gone, the chapel, the post office, the school. They're private houses now. My friend calls it the forgotten village. I only go now to tend the graves. (Interview)

The 'living memories' gathered in the area became the basic material for April's *A Warwickshire Testimony* which itself now stands as a testimonial to past and present lives.

Alison Sutcliffe, Director
July 1999

Clifford Notes compiled by Mrs Avril Salmon and published in the Parish Newsletter. Reprinted by kind permission. All other testimonials reprinted here by kind permission of the individual writers.

We would like to thank the many people whose memories of village life in the early part of the century form the basis of this play. The testimonies from which we have quoted are those of:

Celia Barratt
Mr Cecil Bloxham
Mrs Ethel Clark
Lady Flower
Lady Hamilton
Mrs Peggy Payne
Mr Martyn Richards
Ms C. A. Richers
Mrs Winifred Riley
Mrs Roberts
Mrs Avril Salmon
Mrs Judy Turner
Mrs Connie Turville
Susan Walker

Alcester and District History Society
Kineton and District Local History Group

A Warwickshire Testimony was first performed by the
Royal Shakespeare Company at The Other Place,
Stratford-upon-Avon, on 4 August 1999. The cast was as
follows:

George Antony Byrne
Gladys, Squire Mary Duddy
Dorothy Susan Dury
Tom Derek Hutchinson
Young Edie Catherine Kanter
Diggie, Soldier-Tramp Fergus O'Donnell
Old Edie Cherry Morris
Margery, Mrs Betteridge Alison Reid
Young Gladys, Sandra, Pregnant Woman Sirine Saba

Directed by Alison Sutcliffe
Designed by Paul Farnsworth
Lighting designed by Simon Kemp
Music by Corin Buckeridge
Sound by Andrea J Cox
Movement by Sian Williams
Music Director Michael Tubbs
Dialect Coach Charmian Hoare
Company Voice Work Lyn Darnley and Andrew Wade
Production Manager Mark Graham
Costume Supervisor Louise Dadd

Stage Manager Maggie Mackay
Deputy Stage Manager Pip Horobin
Assistant Stage Manager Thea Jones

Characters

Old Edie
Young Edie
Gladys, Edie's mother
Margery, Edie's sister
George, Margery's husband
Dorothy, Margery's daughter
Tom, Dorothy's husband
Squire
Soldier
Diggie
Mrs Betteridge (Hilary)
Sandra
Pregnant Woman

The crowd scenes are played by the cast

Part One

ONE

The set is absolutely minimal. Dorothy sits alone in a chair. She has a gun on her lap, an old thing you might see about a farm. Tom enters.

Tom Hello love.

He walks straight past her and does not see the gun. He whistles.

Kettle's not on then?

She doesn't answer.

Cup of tea? (*He notices the gun.*) What have you got that out for? Are you sorting through stuff?

Pause.

Dorothy I was about to do myself in.

Tom I beg your pardon.

Dorothy I've made up my mind, Tom. Don't come near me. (*She picks up the gun.*)

Tom Look, look. Now come on. Things aren't as bad as that.

Dorothy Don't tell me how bad things are.

Tom No-one's used that old thing in years, Dorothy.

Dorothy I did last week.

Tom You did?

Dorothy I shot a bird.

Tom A bird.

Dorothy I didn't think I'd hit it but I wanted to try. I thought if I can do it to a bird I can do it to myself. So now you know.

Tom I see.

Dorothy Yes.

Tom So where's me note?

Dorothy What note?

Tom Me flippin' note. When you kill yourself you leave your husband a note. Telling him you loved him and it's not his fault. Telling him how to cook a pork chop.

Dorothy I didn't leave a note.

Tom Bloody selfish to the last.

Dorothy What's the point of a note at a time like this.

Tom Put that antiquated old lump of junk down.

Dorothy I've thought this out, Tom. I am not leaving here and that is that.

Tom Well, you have to. The lease is up. The builders are booked and we are out. Finished.

Dorothy This is my home. This was my grandmother's home.

Tom There's nothing we can do. Now, come on. Give that to me, Dorothy. It belongs in a museum.

Dorothy No, Tom.

Tom You'll have to shoot me then because I'm going to take it. And I know you won't because we've been happily married for thirty-eight years.

Dorothy Don't count on it.

Tom Oh but I am.

Pause. He reaches for the gun. She points it directly at him.

What's happened to all your plans? That book you were going to do for the WI? And Edie'll miss your visits. Won't she? What'll I tell her?

Dorothy You don't understand, do you? The advantage of being dead is that you don't have to worry about anything.

Tom Aim for the heart, Dot. Round about here. (*He points to his chest.*)

Dorothy They're wiping us away, Tom, and you're just standing there letting them do it. Why don't you do something?

Tom What? Kill myself you mean?

Dorothy Something!

Tom I don't see what else I can do, D, except pin my hopes on a future.

Dorothy What bloody future?

Tom We don't own this place, Dorothy. We just live here.

Dorothy There won't be a post office in this village once we go. Think of that. People have bought stamps here since 1899. Till today that is.

Tom I know, love.

Dorothy Why can't they all just go away. Leave us how we've always been.

Tom Things have changed, that's all.

Dorothy Why? Why do things have to change?

Tom Come on Dorothy love. Give us that. (*He indicates gun.*) I've had it now, D. This has gone far enough.

Dorothy What has?

Tom This bloody game you're playing.

Dorothy Is it a game?

Tom takes the gun.

Tom That book. Local history. You should do it. Then it's all set down in print. No-one can wipe that away. They sell those books at the town hall. I bet you fifty pounds you won't finish it.

Dorothy I can see through you, don't think I can't.

Tom Fifty pounds take it or leave it.

He exits. She follows him out.

TWO

Young Edie and Margery enter. They recite the poem together as if to an audience.

We stood at the steps of my dear old home
A fragrant moonlit night in June
The family had gone to the hall to dine
And we two were left alone.

Now what shall we do? I said to my friend
The night is too lovely to stay indoors
Let's go for a walk to the Aston Bend
And look for the ghost that wanders there.

A legend was told by the village folk
Of how long ago a very poor maid
Had killed her child, she was so afraid
Of the taunts and jeers and the hard things said.

And even now after many years
When the moon is full and the shadows lie deep
This maid steals over the grass-grown lane
With her babe in her arms as if asleep.

So off we sped through the quiet night
Past the cottages up the hill
Down again to the four crossroads
Where we stopped and gazed it was so still.

Then suddenly we both of us saw
A shadowy form steal over the road
With her head bent down o'er her burden light
But as if she carried a heavy load.

Oh look! Did you see? Yes, we both had seen
The passing across of the poor lone soul
Who disappeared in the shadows deep
Away to her nameless unknown goal.

Margery This poem was written by Miss Edie Cox and recited by Miss Margery Cox and –

Edie Miss Edie Cox.

They bow. Exit.

THREE

Evening, a country lane.
   George enters. Rests. He has been walking.
   Young Edie trudges on holding a cushion. George watches.

George Hello.

Edie Who's that? Oh, it's you.

George Hello Edie. Where are you off to?

Edie Loan Auntie Gracie this. (*Shows cushion.*) There's a picture showing at the town hall. I don't know why she can't sit on her own fat bum.

George Is she up at Ulveston?

Edie No, she's on Mars. Auntie Gracie is a blinkin' Martian.

George All the way there and back, that's a long way.

Edie And it's not helping talking to you.

George Hasn't Aunty Gracie got her own cushion?

Edie They just like sending me on errands.

George Your mum and Margery?

Edie They just want me out of the way when you call. 'George is coming, take that cushion on a three mile walk.'

George I'm sure that's not true.

Edie Nobody believes a thing I say. I might as well keep me mouth shut. I wanted to learn the violin and when I said that Margery had the violin and I had to learn piano.

George I'll walk with you if you like.

Edie What for?

George Keep you company. It's getting dark.

Edie What about Margery?

George She won't mind. She wouldn't like to think of you out here all alone.

Edie Yes she would. She'd love it. I don't know what you see in Margery.

George She's a very nice girl.

Edie You wouldn't say that if she was your sister. You'd see the true side of her.

George You should say nice things about your sister, Edie. Otherwise it makes you look like a mean person.

Edie So. Nobody likes me anyway.

George They do.

Edie They don't. I've got legs like a carthorse and Margery's got legs like a racehorse.

George Margery does have nice legs.

Edie I hate me. I wish I had long nails then I'd stick 'em in me face and drag 'em down. Finish off the job that God started.

George You're a very dramatic girl.

Edie Is that good or bad?

George And you don't want to do anything to your face, Edie. You've got a nice face.

Edie No I haven't.

George You're not the best judge.

Edie No-one ever said that before. About my face.

George Well, I'm sure they will in the future.

Edie Who will?

George Your young man. When you get one.

Edie I'll never get one. They all like Margery, not me. They want to kiss her not me.

George They do want to kiss you.

Edie You don't.

George Well, I want to kiss Margery.

Edie Kiss me.

George What?

Edie I won't tell Margery. I promise.

George You can't just go around asking men to kiss you, Edie.

Edie Why not?

George They might get the wrong idea.

Edie I just want to know what it's like. I'll close my eyes and pretend it's not you.

George I'd rather you kept them open, thanks. (*He kisses her.*)

George Satisfied.

Edie Yes, that was alright. Least I can say I've been kissed now.

George Well don't let on it was me.

Edie 'Course not. (*She watches him go. She picks up her pillow and hurries off.*)

FOUR

Tom and Dorothy visit Edie in an old people's home.

Tom Hello Edie. It's Tom and Dorothy.

Edie I hate it here.

Tom Do you? It's nice and warm.

Edie I hate the people.

Dorothy What's wrong with them?

Edie They're old.

Tom You're old, Aunty Edie.

Edie Only 82. When I went to get change for my eggs there was a French coin in it. I'm not completely blind. She thought I wouldn't notice but I did. I told her. I want my ten pence. I don't know what you mean, she said. Small minded, see. This is the woman that sells eggs. Room 7. Well, she can stick her eggs from now on. I'll do without.

Dorothy Must be different from the old days. In the village people had to share to get by.

Edie What she want ten pence for? She's not going anywhere. No-one visits her. She's too smelly.

Tom Dorothy's got a plan, Edie.

Dorothy I can tell her, Tom. I'm going to write a book.

Tom And you're going to be in it, Edie.

Dorothy Your stories.

Tom It's Dot's new thing. Her book. She needs something. She's been a bit depressed about the move.

Dorothy Alright Tom.

Edie Well, don't go taking pills for it, Dorothy. My friend did that. They found her in Coventry with no knickers.

Dorothy I've started to make notes. Things I remembered you saying before. How your Gran used to reckon to shoe her twelve children on the money she got blackberrying and the most she ever got was three farthings a pound.

Tom The one about the post office.

Dorothy I know. Nineteen thirty-two. Mrs Arthur Smith helping out at the post office and some money went missing. Newspaper burned in the drawer to look as if it was notes.

Dorothy *and* **Tom** She had the money.

Edie Crafty cow.

Dorothy All that'll disappear. Gone when you go, Edie. Fifteen-seventy the post office cottage is. They dated it by the beams. Ship's beams they were once. Imagine the sights that ship has seen – it's in the wood. The men heading out to sea and the women waiting for them.

Edie Maybe they were glad to see the back of them.

Dorothy 'Course not. They're making us leave. Forcing us out 'cos we don't own it. But I was born there. You know the street you were born. What would you say it was called?

Edie Grump Street.

Dorothy That's right. Grump Street. They're calling it Crabmill Lane now. But it's not Crabmill Lane.

Edie No, it's Grump Street.

Dorothy But Crabmill Lane will sell better. See. They're making up a village and plonking it on top of the old one. It'll be like a grave with the wrong headstone.

Tom So Dorothy's writing a book. It's her way of doing something. She thought she could visit you twice a week.

Edie I'd like that.

Tom Good, that's arranged then. So I'll drop D off next Tuesday, two o'clock.

Edie Are you going already?

Tom We just popped in for today.

Edie Did I ever tell you about the boy who could predict things? Diggie Wheeler. The lad who was hit on the head by the tree that crashed through the roof and after that his mum always said he could predict things.

Dorothy That's a great story.

Edie It was a great tree.

Tom Dot'll hear that one next time. I'm back off to work you see.

Edie I remember everything you know from when I was three days old.

Tom I'll bet you do.

Dorothy 'Bye Edie.

They exit, leaving Edie alone.

Edie It's only my eyes that have gone or I wouldn't be here.

FIVE

Tramp holding his begging cap in hand. He is an ex-First World War soldier.
A group of young people watch.
He sings a fragment of the same song Edie and Margery sang. He approaches with his cap.

Soldier Come on kids.

Young Person 1 He's cracked.

Young Person 2 You're cracked.

Young Person 3 We're not to talk to you.

Young Person 4 Where do you live?

Soldier Round about.

Young Person 1 I've seen his truck.

Young Person 2 A little truck.

Young Person 3 He makes it into a camp with bits of things.

Soldier Did you like the song?

Young Person 1 He cooks over a fire.

Soldier I know another one.

Young Person 2 We ain't got nothing.

Soldier Nothing?

Young Person 3 Were you in France?

Soldier I was in France.

Young Person 2 Why don't you get a job then. The war's over years back.

Young Person 3 He can't he's cracked.

Young Person 1 Edie's dad was in France.

Edie Did you know him?

Soldier No.

Edie Phillip his name was.

Soldier No. There was a lot of us. In different places.

Young Person 1 Phillip's dead isn't he?

Edie Yes. He wrote a letter. He said he liked the mince pies and God bless little Edie 'cos he'd never seen me. Love Phillip.

Young Person 2 But his head got blown off then didn't it?

Edie Yes.

Young Person 3 That's why often we let Edie be the pig in the pig game, don't we?

Edie Yes. And they never found his head.

The soldier sings a verse in a way that suggests he is trying to block out other memories. It is slightly frightening and the children run off.

Soldier
And even now after many years
When the moon is full and the shadows lie deep
This maid steals over the grass-grown lane
With her babe in her arms as if asleep.

He collects his few things, leaves.

SIX

A young woman (Gladys) with a baby in the woods by a frozen pond. She shushes the baby.

Woman Shh, shh. (*She places the baby down. She seems distracted. She hears a whistle.*) Who's there? Is that you? Is that you?

An older woman enters, the Squire. She has a cloak and sensible shoes and short hair. She carries a switch.

Squire Hello there.

Silence. The woman regards her. Then moves on her way, distracted.

Don't tell me. It'll come in a minute. You're one of the Salmon girls. I've known you, well, since you were as small as that one there. Is it a boy or a girl? (*She looks. Picks up the baby.*) She's beautiful. What's her name?

Pause.

Woman Edie.

Squire Your father used to bring you up to the hall at Christmas. He still does the gardens. I'm very particular about my gardens and he's quite excellent. We've had a few rows of course but that's only what one would expect from a decent gardener. Do you remember who I am?

Woman Yes. You're the lady squire.

Squire I remember your wedding. The church looked very pretty. I expect your father helped out there, didn't he? The lovely boughs and the primroses. We were all very shocked to hear the news. Saddened. Phillip was a very decent young man. We all could see there was a lot of love there, between you. It was a terrible war but we must be thankful now it's over.

Pause.

I'm walking the dog. She's probably off after some rabbits. Shall we walk back together?

Woman No. I'm not going back yet.

Squire I'm just thinking it's getting rather cold.

Woman I'm waiting for someone.

Squire They wouldn't want you waiting here. It looks like snow. The pond's frozen, see.

Woman I'm alright.

Squire We don't want the baby getting a chill.

Woman I don't think it is my baby.

Squire Oh yes, yes, I think it is. I can see very clearly that it is.

Woman It cries all the time.

Squire Yes, I see. Why don't you come with me. I'll walk back down to the village with you.

Woman I'm waiting for my husband. I don't think he'd like it if I left. I said I would wait.

Squire He's not coming today.

Woman He'll come. There I heard something.

Squire That's Maddy, the dog.

Woman It sounded like footsteps. This is where we always met.

Squire No-one. Come along. Not today. Really, you can't stay out here.

Woman (*calls*) Phil. Phil! I'll come again soon. I'll wait.

They exit.

SEVEN

Tom enters with pregnant woman.

Tom There's a lady here to see the house.

Dorothy Post office.

Pregnant Woman (*pause. She looks around.*) Beams! He said there'd be beams. Sorry. I'm a little early. I was supposed to meet the man from Howard's here at two.

Tom Would you like a cup of tea?

Pregnant Woman That's very kind.

Dorothy Tom's dad was German.

Tom What's that supposed to mean?

Dorothy It's true isn't it? His dad was a POW. They kept them round here working on the farms. That's how his mum and dad met.

Pregnant Woman That's a lovely story.

Dorothy They'd have strung him up by the balls if they'd have found out.

Tom My wife's doing some research. Local history.

Pregnant Woman I'm sure there's a lot of that. It says in the details that the village is noted for its peace, relaxed pace and the proximity of a large store in a major supermarket chain.

Tom That'll be Sainsbury's.

Pregnant Woman It is exactly what we're looking for.

Dorothy An instinct for obeying orders.

Tom What's that?

Dorothy The Germans.

Tom Yes, thank you, Dorothy.

Pregnant Woman Look. Don't worry about the tea. Do you mind if I just take a look round.

Tom Go ahead.

Pregnant Woman I've really got a tremendously good vibe about this place. The steps.

Tom The steps?

Pregnant Woman Yes. On the way in. Worn into a groove by countless feet. It's quietly moving isn't it? I know this will sound stupid but ever since I've been pregnant things have affected me differently. I've been emotional. Things like that step touch me. And the city. The smell of traffic makes me want to throw up. The other day someone ran over our cat. They just ran her over and left her, and later John, my husband, found her lying by the side of the road her fur soaked in blood and he spoke to her but it was all too late. And I said to him why didn't they just stop the car and come and tell us. She had her collar on with her name and address clearly marked. Its all so anonymous and awful. And then when I stepped in here I felt a weight lift off me. I felt happier than I have done in weeks. I just feel tremendously at home here. We live in Birmingham you see. But my husband's prepared to commute.

Tom Yes, well, we've been very happy here.

Dorothy I was born here.

Pregnant Woman I'll start through there, shall I? (*She exits.*)

Tom So, what's with all the German-bashing?

Dorothy Would you like a cup of tea? She's stealing our home! She's part of it. You'll be offering her bloody flowers next.

Tom Shh.

Dorothy I can shout in my own house if I want.

Tom So what have you got to go dragging my dad into it for?

Dorothy I was angry.

Tom He was a farmer. He never wanted to go to war. Poor sod.

Dorothy You don't have to be nice to her.

Tom He was obeying orders. But so were your lot. They'd be shot if they didn't

Dorothy Not our lot. They wouldn't have got shot. Not that war. Only the war before.

Tom Pick hairs.

Pregnant woman re-enters

Pregnant Woman The view from upstairs is wonderful. Over the trees. It's a sweet room. Your daughter's?

Dorothy Yes.

Pregnant Woman I guessed. I don't know what's happened to the man from Howard's.

Dorothy He's been abducted by aliens, hopefully.

Tom We're a bit sore on the subject of moving.

Pregnant Woman I see. I think perhaps I'll wait outside.

Tom That might be best.

Pregant woman exits.

Dorothy But you'll never be able to buy what we have because you can't buy belonging to a place.

Tom For goodness sake. There's no need to be plain rude.

Dorothy Whose side are you on?

Tom I'm not.

Dorothy Sometimes you have to take sides to stay human.

EIGHT

A parlour. A dead man lies with a sheet over him. Young Edie, her mum Gladys, and the dead man's daughter, Hilary, sit talking.

Hilary We put him on the big table.

Gladys I always think the parlour's the best place. Out of the way of the kitchen.

Edie He's dead.

Gladys Edie's laying out with me today. It's her first time.

Hilary Well, I'm sure Dad would be pleased. Biscuit Edie? (*She offers her from a tin.*)

Gladys Well, what do you say?

Edie Thank you, Mrs Betteridge. (*She takes one gingerly.*)

Hilary Call me Hilary.

Edie Yes, Mrs Betteridge.

Gladys She's not with us half the time, Hilary.

Hilary She's a nice old-fashioned sort of girl, isn't she? Not like my Jenny.

Gladys Don't I get offered a biscuit?

Hilary laughs and offers Gladys one. She tries one.

Gladys These are very nice. Hilary made them specially, Edie.

Edie Oh lovely.

Gladys Funeral biscuits aren't they, Hilary?

Edie looks dismayed. Can't bring herself to eat the biscuit.

Hilary He was a great one for biscuits. I just went up yesterday morning. I said, 'Dad, Dad?' No answer. I thought that's strange. I'd heard him coughing in the night. I called out, 'You alright, Dad?' 'Go to sleep, Hil,' he said. So I did. That was his last words. 'Go to sleep, Hil.'

Gladys He'll get a good wash.

Hilary Oh yes, he'd like that.

Gladys What do you want on him?

Hilary He's got his uniform. I thought he could go in that.

Gladys He'll look smart in that. Mr Bagnall went in silk stockings, there was nothing else available.

Hilary I can't imagine him in those.

Gladys Well, he wasn't about to argue. At the funeral they all stood about like posts trying to think of something nice to say about him. Finally one of them says, 'He was always a good speller.'

Hilary I hope someone comes out with better for me when I go. I've been polishing these pennies. (*Hands over two pennies.*)

Gladys Perfect. They've got a nice shine on them. See that, Edie.

Edie Oh yes. Lovely.

Hilary Poor Dad. I can't believe he's gone. I keep expecting him to pop his head up and say, 'Is there a brew going?' I just can't seem to imagine him not being here.

Edie Lady De Broke still knocks on her husband's door every afternoon, 'cos that's when they always had tea. He's been dead four years. Our Margery told us. She works up there.

> *Gladys gives Edie a look.*

Gladys Edie!

Hilary Dad looked after the horses there years back. He was very good with them. (*She is close to tears.*)

Gladys It would be a great help if you sorted out his uniform, Hilary.

Hilary Yes, yes of course.

Gladys And you might find it needs a bit of pressing.

Hilary I'll put an iron on the fire. (*She exits.*)

Gladys Now I'm going to give Hilary a hand. You start washing him down.

Edie Aren't you going to do it with us?

Gladys It's just giving him a wash. You must know how to do that?

Edie I thought you'd do some of the bits.

Gladys Don't be soft, Edie.

Edie Don't leave me with him.

Gladys For god's sake pull yourself together. Hilary will hear you.

Edie I can't help it. I'm scared.

Gladys There's nothing to be afraid of in a dead body. How are you going to learn if you don't try it?

Edie Are his eyes open?

Gladys Hilary will have closed them, I expect. Now remember what I told you. A good wash all over with a soft rag and then a dry with a towel. Pennies on the eyes. Book under the chin. Cork up his back passage.

Edie Mum!

Gladys Mum nothing. And finish that biscuit. All of it.

> *Edie puts biscuit in her mouth and chews, swallows. Gladys exits. Edie approaches the corpse with trepidation.*

Edie (*whispers*) Mr Handy. Mr Handy. I have to give you a wash. So what I'm going to do is to just start with your head.

She peels back the sheet to just show his face. Edie gives a gasp.

Your eyes are open!

At this moment the 'corpse' comes to life. It is the soldier/tramp but he looks very pale, weird. Edie gasps.

Soldier Is that my little Edie? Haven't you grown?

Edie Is that you, Dad?

Soldier Look at that. Look at you. I'm very cold Edie, very cold.

Edie Well, put the sheet round you.

Soldier You're a thoughtful girl, aren't you?

Edie Not always.

Soldier Is there still them three big trees down Bennet's field?

Edie Oh yes. We have a picnic there every May Day. Margery was the May Queen.

Soldier And dancing?

Edie I wish you never died. I wish I'd seen you. Even once.

Soldier Wasn't to be.

Edie Nobody likes me. You would've done, wouldn't you?

Soldier Give us a hug, eh, Edie?

Edie gives him a hug. He lies back down.

Gladys comes back in.

Gladys What do you think you're doing? I can't leave you alone for five minutes, can I?

Edie He was talking. He was me dad.

Gladys Have you gone off your head?

Hilary enters with uniform.

Hilary There's a button come off. I can't seem to thread the needle. My hands are a bit shaky.

Gladys You leave that to me. (*She takes uniform. To Edie*) Start washing him down. (*Exits.*)

Hilary I'll give you a hand shall I?

Edie stands, unable to do anything.
Hilary begins to wash the dead man's face.

Edie I'm sorry Mrs Betteridge. His eyes . . .

Hilary That's alright, Edie. Dad's not going to know about it, is he?

Edie I can't do anything.

Hilary Are you going to work up at the big house like your sister?

Edie I help Mum out at the post office and I'm learning this.

Hilary I'm sure you'll pick it up with your mum's help. Your mum's a very clever woman.

Edie I know. She delivers babies and all.

Hilary You're probably like your dad. You're like me. I'm like me dad. (*about her dad*) We're making you nice and smart, Dad. Have you got a young man, Edie?

Edie No.

Hilary Not got your eye on anyone?

Edie I'm not allowed to bring trouble into the house till I'm twenty-one or else me mum will kill us.

Hilary How old are you?

Edie Twenty-one. She'll still kill us all the same though.

Hilary Ever thought of doing something with your hair?

Edie I'm not worth bothering over, Mrs Betteridge.

Hilary Well, that's just nonsense, Edie. Everyone's worth bothering with.

Edie I can't do things. I can't do this now. I've let me mum down.

Hilary Maybe if you found something you liked doing then you'd be good at it. My Jenny is a typist in Stratford.

Edie How did she manage that?

Hilary She got a bike.

Edie A bike?

Hilary Cycled to college.

Edie Oh, I might like that. A typist.

Gladys enters carrying uniform.

Gladys Edie?

Hilary I was just helping out, Glad.

Gladys I've sewed his button on. You put that bowl down now, Edie.

Hilary I'm fine sponging him.

Gladys He needs his uniform ironed, Hilary. That's your job. He's going to be a smart soldier. Boer War, weren't it? Very smart.

Gladys hands Hilary uniform.

Dry him, Edie. Start on his top half.

Hilary I'll get on with this, then. (*She exits.*)

Edie picks up the towel.

Edie I can't do it.

Gladys How are you going to get on in life?

Soldier I could be a typist. If I had a bike.

Gladys You were born soft, Edie Cox. (*She addresses the corpse.*) What am I going to do with her?

Soldier You ought to be nicer to Edie, Glad.

Gladys Is that you again, Phil?

Soldier It's always me, ain't it?

Gladys Oh, yes, it's you forever.

Soldier Well, what do you say?

Gladys I'm sorry. I can't help myself. When you were lost all the love got smashed out of me.

Soldier Not even a drop left for little Edie?

Gladys Not even a drop.

Soldier Well, that's sad.

Gladys But life has to go on. Pass us the cork, Edie.

Edie I think I'm going to be sick.

She rushes out.

NINE

Crowd gather for pig killing. The following lines are shared between crowd.

Crowd It knows. The pig knows. That's why it's squealing. What a fantastic pig. She let it sleep downstairs in front the fire in winter. It thinks it's human. It'll all be over quick piggy. Where's Darkie Mullins, pig sticker? Hurry up Darkie, we can't hardly hold it. It's a canny piggy. We want roast pork. We want the trotters for puppets. Brain on toast. Skin for scratchins. It's blood for sausages. A salted haunch for winter. Bacon for breakfast. My mouth's watering. We'll use everything bar the squeak.

Edie I feel sorry for it. Poor pig. What's it ever done to you.

Crowd You want to watch out out, Edie Cox, someone might mistake you for piggy.

Someone makes snuffling noises round Edie.

Let's light the fires down Tippet's field.

Edie hurries away.

TEN

Young Edie appears with battered bag. Margery in maid's uniform.

Margery Edie? What are you doing here?

Edie I've run away.

Margery The housekeeper's gone to mop night. They're killing a pig. I'm having a cigarette. Want one?

Edie You don't smoke.

Margery No?

Edie Did a lad teach you?

Margery You're such a kid.

Edie Does her ladyship know?

Margery When the cat's away. Even when she's here. She walks about like she's looking out to sea. We have to say things three times.

Edie I'm never going back, Margery. I hate her. Mother. I don't even like you much but I couldn't think of anybody else to tell.

Margery Ta very much. Where are you going?

Edie Coventry for all you know.

Margery Mum's a witch. She'll find you.

Edie She won't find me. She's not a witch.

Margery She can touch your hair and tell if you're having a baby.

Edie I'm not scared of her.

Margery Anyway it's good you're here. We're having a bit of a dance.

Edie Who is?

Margery Me and George and Diggie. He's the under gardener. He's going to tell my fortune.

Edie He's not?

Margery He had a bump on the head once, now he can tell the future.

Edie Do you think you should let him?

George and Diggie enter.

George Who's this? Orphan Annie?

Margery Edie's run away. So far she's done a mile.

Edie That's just for starters.

Margery This is Diggie.

Diggie Hello.

Edie Hello.

George What you going to do then, Edie?

Edie I haven't decided.

Margery No rush, you got half an hour.

Edie I might be a typist or work in a hat shop.

Margery Your hem's hanging down. You look like a turnip. Who'd employ you?

George We're just teasing.

Margery Put on the gramophone, Edie, so we can dance.

Edie does so. George dances with Margery. Edie with Diggie. Diggie does very odd dancing.

Edie He doesn't dance properly.

Margery Sit down then. (*She does some spectacular dancing. Stops. Laughs.*)

George Look at Dig. His eyes are popping out his head.

Margery Come over here, Diggie. Now, you know never to tell a lie, don't you?

Diggie Oh yes. But I need a bit of drink.

Margery Like hell.

Diggie I do. To get me going.

Margery gets a bottle out.

Edie Bloody hell, Margery.

Margery Lady De Broke only has it at Christmas.

Diggie takes drink. Drinks it down in one. Sits down quickly.

Diggie I need atmosphere. Shadows. The spirits don't come unless there's shadows.

Edie What spirits?

Margery Don't be daft, spirit spirits.

Edie Oh Margery.

Margery Turn down the lamps, Edie.

Edie does so.

Diggie Give us your hands.

Edie Don't do it, Margery.

George It's alright, Edie. I'm here to protect her.

Diggie I will now listen out for me voices.

Diggie closes his eyes. Starts to move his head as if listening to unseen voices.

Edie What's he doing?

Margery Shhh. Shut up.

After a bit he opens his eyes.

Diggie It's not working.

Margery Why not?

Diggie I think I need another drink.

Margery Get on with it.

Diggie You can't order spirits, Marge Cox. You can't be angry with them.

Margery Why not?

Diggie 'Cos they're bigger than us. Stronger.

Edie How big?

Diggie You can't boss them. Sometimes you can feel them sucking at you. Like they want to suck your brain out your ears.

Margery Have you ever seen one?

Diggie Once I saw a cow with no head. Walking down Pig Brook.

Edie How could it see where to go?

Diggie It was a spirit cow, dumbo.

Margery Here, have this.

She hands him bottle. Diggie drinks it down. He closes his eyes. Listens again. Then he falls asleep.

George He's asleep!

Margery Sly sod! He just wanted to get his hands on the whisky.

George Well, I tell you what I think. Give us your hands, Marge.

She does.

I can see the future. Well would you believe it?

Margery What?

George I find some treasure. I'm digging near the village cross and I find all this Roman treasure. And I'm quite a rich man now.

Margery Who's your wife.

George Didn't I mention that? You, you are. And here's a sexy bit. We've got quite a few little Georges and Margeries running about. And I'm so rich I buy this house. And we are in fact Lord and Lady Not So Broke.

Edie What about me?

George You, Edie? You get a job in a hat shop and live happily ever after.

Edie smiles at him. Diggie begins to whimper.

Edie What's he doing now?

Margery I don't know.

Whimpering gets louder.

Edie Why is he making that noise?

Margery Maybe that's what he does.

Diggie seems scared and backs away. His noises are louder.

Edie Maybe they're sucking his brains out?

Margery Is that what happened to you?

Diggie makes a loud cry.

Edie That can't be right, Margery.

George Dig? Digs? Are you okay?

Diggie makes a more terrified cry which scares even Margery.

Edie Oh God, Marge what have you done?

Margery Shut up. No-one asked you to come.

George What is it, Dig?

Diggie I don't want to say.

Margery Say!

Diggie Fires. That's what they're saying to me and blood. And noise, a terrible smashing, tearing as loud as a ship ripped in half. And sadness like a big black hole swallowing everything. Swallowing the village and all.

Margery He's drunk. That's the trouble.

Diggie My head's on fire with it. Dead faces with horror in their dead eyes floating in a sea of fire.

Margery He's making it up.

She grabs him, shakes him.

Diggie A great rumbling noise and screams and bodies, I think they are, hanging from hooks and blood gushing out.

Margery You half-wit. (*Hits Diggie.*) He's drunk the silly sod. You scared the living daylights out of us.

Edie Maybe it's the pig roasting and that on his mind.

George That'll be it.

Diggie It ain't that. It ain't that. Too many, too many.

Margery When that tree fell on your head it should have finished you off. Take him home Edie, on your way back.

Edie But I've run away.

Margery I don't know which of you is softer. Go on. Go home. I've got to sort this room out.

George I'll see him back.

Margery No need for you to go yet. Let Edie take him.

Edie exits with Diggie. They get caught up in the crowd.

ELEVEN

Crowd gather for pig killing. The following lines are shared between crowd.

Crowd Hold her tighter! Tighter. She's seen Darkie. She's seen his knife. Her eyes are wild. She screams. How quick his knife slices her. Blood gushes out.

Pump its leg to drain its heart. Every last drop. Get the kids to jump on her.

That gets the blood out. They've lit the fire. Drag it there. Roast the delicacies. Hang the rest in the big tree till morning.

Crowd disperses.

Edie I can't help feeling sorry for it. You alright now?

Diggie nods his head.

Edie Do you think Margery's pretty?

Diggie Yes.

Edie Don't you know anything?

Diggie What?

Edie You're not supposed to say that are you? And what about me?

Diggie Well, you're friendly.

Edie I don't want to be friendly. I want to be pretty. Will you come somewhere with me?

Diggie Where?

Edie Up the hill.

Diggie What for?

Edie I don't want to be a virgin any more. None of the girls round here are except me. Why's that? I want to be able to shout it out to me mum. Into her face. I am not a virgin. Just to see her face. To show her. Coming?

Diggie Alright.

Edie Will you tell us what it was you saw? Before.

Diggie War, that's what it was.

Edie takes his hand and they exit.

TWELVE

Dorothy, Old Edie. Tom, stands with his car keys, waiting to take Dorothy back.

Dorothy She was telling me about the pig.

Tom What about the pig?

Dorothy How it had a name like Margaret or Bert.

Tom Margaret?

Dorothy It was like one of the family. It's all going in my book. They would've fed it turnips every day, scratched its back with a stick. If your pig died of the purples that was a disaster. That was hunger. The kids cried when it was time to kill the pig. They looked one last time into its sad creasy eyes, rubbed its snout and listened to its snuffling, but they knew it had to go. That was life.

Edie You killed your pig in November, say. All the neighbours had some. Then when they killed their pig in January you had some of theirs. People shared. They had to. Not like her with the eggs in Room Seven

Dorothy You could trust people then. No-one locked their doors, did they? You got your milk from a farm, pulled apples from the trees. You were in a kind of paradise, weren't you?

Tom Sounds like it's going to rain.

Edie Trouble is I don't think I can help you any more.

Dorothy Why not?

Edie My memory. I forget things in here.

Tom You've got a good memory.

Edie It's all leaking out of me, like out of an old bath, and that's the truth, Jim.

Tom Tom.

Edie See, it's terrible.

Dorothy What'll happen to my book?

Tom Have you got those photos, D? Show Edie some of those.

Dorothy does so.

Dorothy Who's that?

Edie I don't know.

Tom That's you, isn't it?

Edie Is it?

Tom With D's mum, Margery. You weren't even looking properly.

Dorothy How about this one?

Edie Bugs Bunny.

Dorothy Edie.

Edie I mean it, Dorothy. A few more weeks in here and I'll start dribbling. Mrs Fisher was dead three days before they stopped wheeling her out for meals. That's because they couldn't tell the difference. She was a lively minded card cheat when she came in here. And I've forgotten the name of her that runs this place.

Dorothy Her with the big hair?

Edie Yes. And the other day I forgot the name of these. (*She points to her feet.*)

Tom Feet.

Edie Yes, I know now. Don't leave me in here.

Tom We'll be out of a home ourselves soon, Edie.

Edie Please don't leave me. Let me come home with you. Just for a day or two. It's being in here that's making me forget. I just look at the walls all day and I'm going blank like the walls. You leave me in here and I'll turn soft and that's a promise.

Dorothy We can't leave her here. She'll have to come back with us for a bit. Poor Edie.

Edie begins to sing. It merges with the next scene.

THIRTEEN

Young Edie alone in the woods. She looks pale, cold.

Edie (*sings*)
Edie Cox is my name
England is my nation
Haselor is my dwelling place
And god is my salvation.

She steps up to 'water's edge'. She closes her eyes and makes as if to step in.
  George appears, watches. He is rolling a fag. He is in soldier's uniform.

George What you doing, Edie?

Edie George! You gave me the fright of my life.

George Going swimming?

Pause.

Well, how are you these days? Do us a favour. Sit with us a bit. Go on. Just while I have this smoke.

He sits down. Edie sits next to him.

That's good. Still asking lads for a kiss?

Edie Why do you say that?

George I was just joking with you. I've been to see Margery up at the manor house. There's going to be soldiers living up there soon. Margery'll have to go.

Edie Do you know where you're going?

George I'll know in two weeks when I finish training.

Edie Maybe you'll go to France?

George Maybe.

Edie Do you want to go?

George Not up to me is it? We had a talk by an officer – about being a soldier. Diggie Wheeler now knows a brothel isn't a soup kitchen.

Edie Have you got a gun, George?

George Why do you want to know?

Edie 'Cos I was going to drown myself but maybe shooting's quicker.

George Why do you want to do that?

Edie It's none of your business.

George It's my gun.

Edie I'm having a baby.

George Are you?

Edie Yes, and if I don't die me mum'll kill me.

George It's a free country.

Edie I don't know why I did it. It was stupid.

George Who's the dad then.

Edie Nobody.

George First time I've heard of that happening.

Edie If you won't help me I'll just have to go into the pond.

George Drowning's a horrible way to die.

Edie Well what else am I supposed to do? I don't think I was supposed to be here. And now I'm doing the same again. Bringing a baby into the world that's not supposed to be here either.

George Only God can say that, Edie.

Edie I don't think there is a God, George.

George What is there then?

Edie I don't know. I'm thick.

Pause

George You know I wish there wasn't a war Edie. I don't want to go. I don't want to leave here. This is my home. I work here. I love it. I hate the thought that something might happen and I might not ever come back. But what I keep thinking is well, I might come back and then all this will be waiting for me. Just like it is. Perfection. You have to think the same, Edie. You're in a bad patch now but you'll come through it and then you can live again, be happy like you were before.

Edie Nobody cares if I live or die.

George I care. I want you here when I get back because you're part of my home. I don't want nothing to change, Edie, not even you. So go home and leave that pond in peace.

He kisses her on the forehead. Gets up. She doesn't move.

George 'Bye Edie.

He goes to leave. Edie suddenly jumps up.

Edie George! George!

He stops.

Edie What if I never see you again.

George Don't say that, it's bad luck.

She runs up to him and kisses him.

FOURTEEN

Old Edie, Dorothy. Tom enters. He has been at work, is dirty.

Tom We had a man brought his car to the garage today I checked it over and it was two cars soldered together. Back half and front half. I told him and he says, 'Is it safe?' I said, 'Put it like this, I can't guarantee that your back seat passengers will arrive at the same destination as the driver.'

Dorothy People used to take pride in what they did. That's why old things have lasted.

Tom I was thinking Edie's had her week now. It's time she went back.

Edie I'm not going back.

Tom It's just the thought of it. It's not so bad when you're there.

Edie Yes it is, it's bloody awful. Anyway I'm not going back because Dorothy says I can stay here.

Tom Does she?

Edie Yes she does.

Tom Is that right Dorothy?

Dorothy Don't start, Tom.

Tom I'm not starting. I'm just making calm enquiries about my living arrangements.

Dorothy It's convenient to have Edie here while I'm working on the book.

Tom There is the small matter of us moving in a fortnight. I suppose you've taken that into consideration. We haven't started packing yet.

Dorothy You don't have to remind me, Tom.

Tom After we've taken Edie back we can discuss it.

Dorothy Edie is staying here. She is not going back to that place. It's a nothing place where you just wait to die. It's not a life there. Nobody knows who you are or what you've done. You disappear first and then you die. It's a sort of miniature Birmingham in fact.

Tom You're not planning a job with West Midlands Tourist Board then?

Dorothy This place lives and breathes history, Tom. Sometimes I get this feeling when I'm out walking and there's no-one else about. Late afternoon it usually is, and the wind's in the trees. I look up and I think I could be in Tudor times, I could be. What's to say I'm not? As if just for a moment I've stepped through some sort of door into the past. And it's beautiful, it really is.

Tom And where am I in all this? Conveniently not yet born for four centuries.

Dorothy I was just trying to explain something. There's more here than there is outside. A beautiful way of life just beyond our reach and you can still feel it if you try hard enough. It's like the old days are real. Realer than what's out there.

Tom We've got to look to the things we do have. We've got each other. I wouldn't choose to leave but you have to see that there might be a positive side to it. You go on about how good the past was but you're forgetting I've heard some of the stories too.

Dorothy You've never really felt the same way about it have you? You'd have left here a long time back, if it weren't for me.

Tom That's not true.

Dorothy This post office was my family's livelihood for a hundred years. You're not rooted here like I am.

Tom It's not the post office. It's Marion.

Dorothy It's not Marion.

Tom 'Course it is.

Dorothy Being here it's a tradition.

Tom Are you going to wait here till the builders convert it round you? No, it's Marion. You never accepted that she was gone. And I never pushed it. That was my mistake. I should have made you face it.

Dorothy They never found any trace of her, Tom.

Nobody vanishes just like that. A lovely girl just like that. Maybe she went to Australia.

Tom What, and one day she's going to just walk through the door?

Dorothy Well, we just don't know do we?

Tom She's dead, love. After seven years it's official.

Dorothy What do they know? One day she could just arrive and what if we're not here?

Tom After twenty years. I don't think so Dorothy.

Dorothy You've given up on her too easily, Tom. That's not love.

Tom She was my daughter too. I loved her just as much as you.

Dorothy Not as much as me. Because I can't leave and you can.

Pause.

Tom There's no point arguing like this. Now, come on. Let's take Edie back.

Dorothy No Tom, no. I'm sorry. It's just not that simple.

Tom (*shouts*) Well, what the bloody hell else can we do?

Pause.

I'm going to stay at the Crown. I'll wait till tomorrow morning and then I'm going. I'll cut straight through all my ties. You, everything. I'm letting go my past before it sucks me down with it. And you'll have to decide if you're coming with me or not. Oh, and one more thing. Please come. (*He exits.*)

Edie Maybe he was right. Maybe you should have taken me back.

Dorothy No. Anyway you said yourself you forgot things in there.

Edie Sometimes it's good to forget things, though, Dorothy, you know that. Me and you both got things we don't want to remember.

Dorothy I love this time of day. Night starting to creep in. The dark cuts you off from the world. I always think of the village all huddled together and round it the dark. It's like an island then. Just like it must have been once.

Edie I didn't like that. Margery didn't like it neither. Margery's dead but look at me – somehow I've ended up back here.

Dorothy Paradise.

Part Two

FIFTEEN

Old Edie alone in cottage. Early morning, still dark.

Edie Blinkin' hell.

What've you done, Edie Cox? How come you're back here? Why spend a lifetime avoiding a place and then end up stuck there in your twilight years? Poor Dorothy. She's not right, is she? She's been through it – losing that child. And living in a village doesn't help. Her nose stuck in the past. Why don't you tell her the truth? People may look all angelic and innocent and fuzzy in those old photos but they could be bastards all the same. Just like now. You've taken advantage of Dorothy, you have. You're a wicked old woman and what are you going to do about it? You no good to anyone. Worse. You're trouble. Dorothy's a good niece. She always brought you your favourite biscuits an' all. Hobnobs, and they're not cheap. This place brings out the worst in you. It hasn't changed. Same doors, same floor. I can see you, Mum, sewing something in the corner. Shrouds probably. That was what you used to make. Four for two bob. And there's Margery drying her stockings in front of the fire. I don't like meeting you all again I can tell you. I can feel you in the shadows waiting to step out. Well, that's not how it's going to be. You can stick to the damp and the corners. I'm shutting me mouth from now on. If I was young I'd leave. Pack me case. Sneak out early one morning when the air is still and the sun just creeping up. Grip the handle of my suitcase. My young feet are quick. Trip trip they go. And then I'm away, free. Best thing I ever did. That was when my life started. Me real life.

SIXTEEN

1960. Edie's hairdressing salon. Edie looks very fashionable: lipstick, heels. Edie is waiting for a family visit. She checks all is in place. Sandra, her assistant, comes in.

Sandra I think they're coming. I seen them coming along the street. Three of them.

Edie Well, it's the right number. Sandra, for goodness sake. You've done your buttons up cockeyed.

Sandra Oh no. I've not have I? (*She fumbles with the buttons.*)

Edie Here. (*She helps her.*)

Sandra Thank you, Miss Cox. I hope I don't let you down.

Edie You won't, Sandra.

Sandra I love this salon. I love working here. It's a bit of class. There was a woman from London in last week. That's the bell. Oh heck, it's them!

Margery, Dorothy and Gladys enter. Gladys is last – sniffy.
Margery holds Dorothy's wedding dress. Dorothy is eighteen. Margery looks about her.

Margery Well!

Edie Margery.

Dorothy Hello, Aunty Edie.

Edie Hello, Dorothy love. It's a big day isn't it?

Dorothy Yes. I can't believe it.

Margery She slept like a log. It was me that had her brain turning over all night.

Edie Mum.

Gladys Edie.

Edie How are you?

Gladys Can't complain.

Edie Sandra.

Sandra Yes, Miss Cox?

Edie Could you see if any of our clients require a coffee?

Sandra Oh yes. Of course. I was forgetting. Standing here like a plank. Does anyone require a coffee?

Gladys No thank you.

Sandra Oh.

Gladys You can't trust the cups in these places.

Margery I'll have one. Why not, if it's going?

Dorothy I couldn't swallow a thing. I've got butterflies.

Edie Chop chop then, Sandra. Then can you do the combs.

Sandra Yes, Miss Cox.

Margery Isn't it lovely here? Very smart. We'll be like three queens when you've finished with us, Edie. You doing well then?

Edie I do manicures an' all.

Margery Do you?

Edie Eyebrow plucking and facials.

Margery Very posh.

Edie There's magazines there to look through. I've had me decor modelled on the interior of the Chanel house in Paris.

Gladys Go down well in Coventry, does it?

Edie You decided what you're having done, Mum?

Margery I fancy a change. Something that when I walk into that church heads swivel.

Dorothy It's my wedding.

Margery Something that'll make your dad take a bit of notice. Maybe you could stick a sign post in saying North Pole 2,000 miles. That should wake him up.

Dorothy Dad's in another world half the time. Tom notices everything.

Margery That'll wear off after six months.

Dorothy It won't. Will it?

Edie No.

Margery They all start out nice lads. They end up as husbands. Farting and snoring and whatnot.

Gladys No need to be crude, Margery.

Edie In the chair then, Dorothy.

Dorothy sits.

Margery What do you think, Edie?

Edie Have you got the veil?

Dorothy I'm not having a veil.

Margery She's having a veil affair. Tulle coming out of a tiara.

Gladys A bit of lace on a hairband.

Dorothy Like Audrey Hepburn in *Roman Holiday*.

Margery Here. (*Pulls veil out of a bag.*)

Edie Lovely.

Edie experiments with Dorothy's hair and veil.

Edie Something like that might work?

Dorothy Oh, ain't that lovely, Mum?

Margery Yes, that's nice. That's nice, isn't it, Mum?

Gladys Looks like a cottage loaf.

Margery We'll have that then. The Hepburn loaf.

Edie Right. That's sorted.

Edie begins to comb through. As she first touches Dorothy's hair, she registers something, continues. Sandra enters with coffee.

Sandra Coffee.

Margery Thanks love.

Sandra I'll do the combs now, shall I?

Edie Thank you, Sandra.

Exits.

Margery Here, she's a bright spark that Sandra.

Edie She's learning. She'll be alright when I've finished with her.

Margery I was just thinking. How long is it since we've all been together like this? Years, isn't it?

Edie Years.

Margery Criminal isn't it? Us just a bus away really.

Edie I always send a card at Christmas.

Margery Well, it's a good day to heal the breach. A wedding day.

Gladys Well, that's the thing, isn't it?

Margery What is?

Gladys If you walk out on your family.

Edie I had to earn me living, Mum.

Gladys What was wrong with the post office and a bit of laying out?

Margery We can put that all behind us now. This is a fresh start.

Edie How's that looking, Dorothy? I'm going to back comb it now. Then put a bit of spray on.

Margery The big house is empty, Mum was saying.

Edie Is it?

Margery No-one wants it now. Can't afford the servants I suppose.

Dorothy Servants! Who'd want to be a servant.

Gladys Nothing wrong with being in service. Your mum was once.

Margery That was in the stone ages, Dorothy.

Gladys Oh yes, everything's gone downhill.

Edie You can't expect people to work for peanuts. Not nowadays.

Margery Oh, I like me wages. The only think about paint is it gives you a bloody headache at the end of the day.

Gladys There was always a party at the manor at Christmas. The Squire gave that. She made sure every child had a present off the tree. Even the soft ones like Edie.

Margery That looks special, Dorothy.

Dorothy Does it?

Margery Lovely.

She kisses Dorothy.

You take after your mum.

Dorothy Oh God. I feel all funny.

Margery How do you mean?

Dorothy I don't know. I feel as if I'm going to burst into tears!

She does so.

Gladys What's the matter with her?

Margery Come on. You'll start me off.

Dorothy This feeling's come over me.

Margery What?

Dorothy I don't know. Like I'm shutting a door and I'll never be able to open it again.

Margery Is that all? That's just life. If I had a pound for every door I've shut. Half the time I've left me shopping on the other side.

Dorothy But I don't like it.

Margery You'll get used to it. Now, stop crying. You're ruining you makeup.

Dorothy calms down.

Go and get your dress on. I'll be in in a minute.

Dorothy exits.

Margery Kids eh? (*She lights up.*) Me now, is it? We haven't got that much time. Just tart me up, Edie. I want to be the most glamorous mother of the bride present.

Gladys You've spoilt that girl, Margery.

Margery Dorothy?

Gladys Nowadays they don't know about life.

Edie What's to know?

Gladys Mods and rockers.

Edie It's just kids wanting a bit of fun.

Gladys One came into the post office and tried to buy a postcard.

Margery It's not illegal.

Gladys I told him, when my Phillip was your age he was dead.

Edie The customer is always right, Mum.

Gladys Not in my shop. It's like they're walking about in a dream and they don't know anything.

Edie Why should they know about horrible things? They're young and they want a bit of a laugh.

Gladys You're not young any more.

Edie Not if you say so, Mum.

Margery (*checks her hair*) That looks smashing. I'm going to see how our Dorothy's doing. (*She gets up. Hurries out.*)

Edie Come on then, Mum. Hop in the chair.

Gladys I've changed me mind. I don't want me hair doing.

Edie It's a treat. It's all on me. It's a special day.

Gladys I said I don't want it doing.

Edie You want to look nice for a wedding, don't you?

Gladys I'll keep me hat on. (*She gets a hat out, puts it on defiantly.*)

Edie I'd like to do it.

Gladys No. I don't want you touching me.

Sandra I done the combs.

Edie Right. Good. Count the towels for me will you, Sandra.

Sandra Righto. (*Exits.*)

Edie Tom and Dorothy are going to be living with you at the post office. That's nice. Dorothy'll be helping out will she?

Gladys It's a little job for her.

Edie I was thinking perhaps I could pay a visit.

Gladys Do what you like.

Edie Alright. I won't visit you. See how you like that.

Gladys I will like it.

Edie Good.

Gladys You've always been contrary. Since you were tiny.

Edie I haven't!

Gladys I tried my hardest with you.

Edie No you never. You never even liked me.

Gladys No. Because you were contrary. I could drop

dead next week and who'd be there to see to me. I'll be handled by strangers.

Edie Mum.

Gladys They won't see to me properly. They'll put me in a bag like an old cat.

Edie Mum!

Gladys And all because you're too selfish to come back home.

Edie I'm not the little mouse you could once push around. I've seen a bit of life.

Gladys So I've heard.

Edie What's that supposed to mean?

Gladys Criminal types picking you up in cars.

Edie News travels fast doesn't it on the bloomin' Warwickshire drums?

Gladys They're not the sort of men that are going to make you happy.

Edie I have a bit of a drink and a dance. There's no harm in that.

Gladys They've probably got wives at home. Haven't they?

Edie Harems I should think.

Gladys Don't be smart with me. You're not happy, I can see that, and you've only got yourself to blame.

Edie I am happy. I was bloody ecstatic till you came.

Gladys This place is a dump. That girl you've got working for you is a fool. You've not come to much, have you? Margery's got a family and a proper home.

You've just been wasting your time here. What use are you to anybody?

Edie I'm earning a living. I don't see how I'm any different from you.

Gladys Once I took you into the woods when you were a baby. It was half in my mind to leave you. I might have done if the Squire hadn't stopped me.

Pause.

Edie What do you want to go telling me that for?

Gladys I never left you, did I? You can't leave things behind no matter what. You can't forget your family.

Edie I'm forgetting them better every day.

Margery enters.

Margery Everybody happy? Come on in, Dorothy. Make a fuss of her.

Dorothy enters.

Margery There. Doesn't she look lovely?

Edie Yes. Lovely.

Gladys She's got rouge on.

Dorothy Here's Dad in the car.

Dorothy exits.

Margery What's happened to you, Gladys? It looks like you've had the Hepburn bap.

Edie She didn't want her hair done.

Margery Bloody marvellous. I can't leave you two alone for five minutes, can I? You'll never be right together you two, will you?

Edie I suppose that's my fault, is it?

Margery Let's not argue eh? If we can't be nice to each other today, when can we? I'm walking round. You coming, Mum? Edie?

Edie I'll lock up here first. Dorothy looks lovely, Marge.

Margery exits. Gladys exits. Edie stands a minute. Dorothy runs back in.

Dorothy I forgot to say thank you.

Edie Don't you worry. Have a lovely day.

Dorothy Thanks, Aunty Edie.

Edie Did you know you were in the family way, Dorothy?

Pause.

Dorothy I'm not, am I?

Edie I can always tell. When I touch the hair.

Dorothy God. I think I'm really happy.

Pause.

You're a witch like Gran.

She exits. Sandra comes in, waves them off.

Sandra Don't she look wonderful? Fifty-seven.

Edie What?

Sandra Towels.

Edie Now we can do the mirrors.

Sandra I thought we were closing early today?

Edie No. I've changed my mind. I'm not going to the wedding.

Sandra Not going!

Edie And I don't want to stand about all day chatting to you. Now get busy!

Sandra Yes, Miss Cox.

Exits. Edie stands a moment and then follows.

SEVENTEEN

Two years later. The salon. George is laying a bit of carpet at the entrance.
Edie comes in.

Edie That's it. Six o'clock. (*She locks the door.*) That looks lovely, George.

Sandra enters.

It looks nice, doesn't it, Sandra?

Sandra Oh yes. It looks absolutely fantastic.

George It'll stay down, anyway.

Sandra I bet it will. I bet it would stay down for a hundred years.

Edie Yes, well, thank you Sandra.

Sandra It's got such a lovely soft feel to it.

George It's a decent bit of carpet.

Edie Now. George. You are not going anywhere till you have a drink.

George Well, I said I'd go over and see our Dorothy tonight and the little lass.

Edie You can have a bit of drink first. Tea, or vodka and lime?

George In a hairdressers?

Edie I work late three nights a week. I finish with a vodka and lime. I deserve it.

Sandra I have one sometimes.

Edie But you're off home tonight aren't you, Sandra?

Sandra Me?

Edie Yes.

Sandra Oh yes. Yes. I'll just get me coat. Well, 'bye then. (*She exits.*)

Edie Drink?

George I won't, thanks.

Edie Well, stay with me while I have one, George. Stop lurking by the door. Sit down.

He sits. She gets herself a drink.

Edie Do you remember that time when I was taking the cushion up to Auntie Gracie?

George The cushion?

Edie You remember.

George Yes, I do.

Edie Let's see what's on the radio. (*She switches it on, finds music.*) I love this. Jack Brady and his orchestra.

George I better go. It's a bit of a drive.

Edie switches off the radio.

Edie You must miss Margery.

George Yes.

Edie I miss her too. Do you remember that time I met you by the pond. You said things. It made me feel better just to stand next to you. It was as if something came off of you. Like a warm feeling. I thought, that man's alive. You sort of woke me up.

George I was just a kid then.

Edie Well, we were all kids.

George When I came back things weren't the same. You can never count on things staying the same.

Edie Things change. I woke up and I left there double quick time, George, I can tell you. And I've never regretted it a day since.

George Haven't you?

Edie No. Why should I? What was my life there? Me and Margery used to sleep in our coats in winter, it was that freezing. One tap between four families. Horrible.

George I remember the birds. Swifts, larks, yellow-hammers.

Edie Well, we remember different things, that's all. If you liked it so much why did you leave?

George Came back from the war. Farms had changed. Big houses gone. No work. I ended up working in the quarries. Forced labour. Still, I was better off than Diggie Wheeler. He was in the abbatoir.

Edie I like working for myself. I've saved quite a bit.

George This is a very nice place.

Edie But somehow I feel I'm missing something.

George You seem fine, Edie.

Edie I've had some scrapes.

She gets out a magazine. Shows it to George.

George (*reads*) *True Life Crimes.*

Edie Page 17. I went out with him for a bit. (*She points to picture.*)

George (*reads*) 'Tall, handsome, young airforce –'

Edie Well, he was dressed as airforce.

George (*reads*) 'Neville Church was a suave sex maniac, one of the most violently depraved men the world has ever known. On a few summer days he haunted England's genteel South Coast.'

Edith He done a chain murder down in Brighton. I knew him for about six weeks. One night I was waiting up St Nicholas Church street for Neville and up come Bernie with her boyfriend. 'Where's Neville,' I says. Bernie's boyfriend got out the car, he says 'Edie, you'll never see him again.' I said, 'Never? Why?' He put his hands on my shoulders, he says, 'Consider yourself a very lucky girl.' And the next fortnight after that he done a chain murder. Then one day he pulled up at the Coventry traffic lights and he says, 'What you looking at, Edie?' I says, 'Your eyes, I've never seen eyes like them'. They were red and blue and white and purple. Do you know what happened? It's perfectly true. He went to kiss me and I belched and he just pushed my head to one side like he used to do before he murdered them and he said, 'Urgh, Edie, what you been eating?' 'Pilchards on toast,' I said, 'I love 'em.' He couldn't get rid of me quick enough. I'm sure that's what saved my life.

George Bloody hell.

Edie I know. That's why I'm looking for someone normal. Someone I can trust.

Pause

I didn't really need a new bit of carpet. I mean it's lovely and all that. I just wanted to see you. You always promised you'd pop round but you never did. Aren't you lonely, George?

George Yes.

Edie You like a pair of arms around you, don't you? Everybody does. You know everything about me, George. All my secrets. It's as if you were there at all the right times. That means something. You've always liked me a bit haven't you?

George Yes.

Edie Well, for goodness sake. We could be much happier together than on our own.

George But I was Margery's husband.

Edie Yes I know.

George Well, it wouldn't be right.

Edie Why not? You can come and live here, over the shop. And in a way it's fair. Margery had half of you and now I can have the other half.

George I'm not a sandwich.

Edie I know.

George Don't you ever feel that everywhere's crowded? Crowded with old things people said. With them.

Edie That's creepy, George. That's like saying we're surrounded by ghosts.

George I feel like that sometimes.

Edie There's no-one here. Just us. Say yes.

Pause. George looks at Edie.

George You always were dramatic.

Edie George. I don't know how to say this. Please be like you were before. Please.

George I don't know how, Edie. I'm like that thing they found. Out of my time.

Edie What thing?

George In the quarry. The dinosaur.

The door opens. Sandra enters.

Sandra Oh, sorry. I'm sorry. But . . .

Edie What is it, Sandra?

Sandra It's him. I found him wandering around again. I didn't know what to do.

Diggie enters in civilian clothes. He has been drinking.

Sandra He hasn't got anywhere to go. He was wondering if he could sleep here again?

George Digs?

Sandra He's been in the pub.

George It's George Lively.

Diggie George?

George How are you doing?

Diggie Not so bad.

Sandra George has been putting in our carpet. It's the most lovely bit of carpet. You could curl up on that carpet.

Edie He keeps turning up here. Don't you Diggie?

Diggie I haven't got any money.

Edie I'm soft. I've given him beer money. You've had your lot off me!

Diggie Loan us two bob, George.

George does so.

Thanks. (*He staggers a bit.*)

Sandra I never meant to interrupt anything. I didn't know where else to bring him.

Diggie Tired.

Sandra He just falls asleep like a baby, doesn't he?

Edie Not tonight he's not, I'm putting my foot down.

George Where will he go then?

Edie I don't care.

George Can't just turn him out on the streets, forget about him.

Edie He can stay with you if he likes.

George I suppose he can.

Diggie I like to be with Edie. Me and you went up the hill. We held hands.

Edie I want you to go away and leave me alone, understand? I'm trying to run a business.

Sandra I'll walk him down the road on my way home. I've got some Polos. I'll give him one of them.

Sandra exits, taking Diggie with her.

Edie So that's a no, isn't it, George.

George I'm sorry. Edie.

Edie It's me, isn't it?

George What?

Edie I'm the one that's stuck in the past. Not you. I'm the bloody dinosaur. Goodbye, George.

George I had better be off. (*He hesitates.*) What happened to the baby Edie?

Edie It wasn't a baby. I just imagined it was.

George You always had an imagination. Well, I must go. Dorothy and all that. Goodbye, Edie.

Edie Goodbye.

George exits. Edie stands for a moment watching him. She gets herself a big drink. Lights a cigarette. Finds some music on the radio – something very contemporary like 'the twist' – turns it up really loud and dances to it while drinking and smoking.

I'm the bloody dinosaur but no bloody longer.

EIGHTEEN

A crowd gathers. They share the dialogue.

Crowd What's it like? How big is it? Bill Morris found it in his lunch break. He saw it sticking out. A great big tooth sticking out of a rock. Maybe it was hungry? Maybe it wanted his sandwich? Maybe it wanted Bill Morris. It must've been desperate. It's from ancient times. Prehistoric it said in the paper. An ichthyosaurus. How many years is prehistoric, Mum? A lot. Is it a million years? One day will a million years have gone by again? Will someone dig up Bill Morris in a million years? He'll be called sandwich man. Here it comes! In that big box. They're winching it out. We want to see the bones and the teeth. It's our blinkin' ichthyosaurus and we want to see it! Taking it away to some museum. Locking it up. They say it had a tail, a great long tail. And there it was all this time sleeping in our quarry.

Crowd disperse leaving Tom and Dorothy, with baby.

NINETEEN

Dorothy It's romantic, isn't it, Tom? They say there must have been forests here and a big lake.

Tom Can I have a kiss?

Dorothy In a minute. No. It's not romantic it's something else.

Tom I'll hold my breath till I get one.

Dorothy It's scary. Time is huge, Tom, isn't it? And we're tiny. We're just like the leaves on a tree that are going to fall off.

Tom Hey, Dot. I'm going to fall into the quarry if you don't kiss me. I'm falling, look.

Dorothy laughs. Kisses him.

Tom Time to go. Opening time one hour.

Dorothy Can't you take the day off?

Tom I can't keep having days off.

Dorothy I know. I just want to sit in the sun with you and the baby.

Tom I'd like to do that too, but I can't.

Dorothy She's beautiful isn't she, Tom?

Tom Like her mum.

Dorothy I'm so happy I feel sad.

Tom How come?

Dorothy I feel so lucky. It can't go on like this, can it?

Diggie enters.

Diggie Oak. Ash. Plane. Birch. Three walnuts grew near here once, but they were chopped down. They took the branches first, so they looked poor sad things before they hacked them down. I saw that. I see things before they come.

Dorothy I don't like him, Tom. He's blocking out the sun.

Tom You be off now, there's a good chap.

Diggie She's a pretty girl.

Dorothy He gives me the shivers.

Tom He's just a tramp.

Diggie There's a man and he's not letting her go.

Dorothy What does he mean?

Tom Nothing. Go on now. Be off.

Diggie stands.

We've got to be off anyway, D. Come on. The beer's got to be put on tap. I promised I wouldn't be late this morning. Why don't you come. Put our Marion out the back and sit in the garden with her. Mrs Hewins won't mind.

Dorothy I'd like that.

Exit both.
Diggie alone in the woods.

Diggie I sleep in this wood sometimes. I sleep where I can. I like the smell of earth. I clear weeds away sometimes but nobody can see. They come back quick enough, but I like the work. In the other place I didn't like it. The bodies came too fast. Swinging towards you another and another. Stab, slit. Stab, slit. Then another. Swinging away, swing towards you. Your feet in the blood. The stink. Pigs screaming, machines shrilling. In twenty seconds they've bled to death. You know what's coming towards you; a death and another and another and your heart shuts off. That's your bit of peace. It's peaceful here. Except when he comes. I don't like to see him. I don't like to see him with the girl. He has her by the arm and he pulls her. She is talking to him all the while but he's not listening. She's a pretty girl. I found an orchid here that's very rare. You don't see them much. Like a single white flame balancing on its stalk. Things have gone. Things you saw every day. Flowers. Primroses. They used to be everywhere. Birds have gone too. It's quieter in the woods. Maybe they all flew away one winter and decided not to come back. I might have done that if I was a bird. She's saying to him to let her go. But he's not. She's white. Her face is white and her hair is stuck to it dark like weeds. He has her by the arm and he's not letting go. He has a coat on like a soldier's so it's harder to make him out, but her white face sticks out. There she is. There's the orchid. She's still there.

He gets down to look.

I could watch her all day. White lady we used to call her. Nobody comes here. Nobody should hurt you. Army green. I can see him now. She fights him but he has a knife. Please stop. Please. Then it gets dark. All the while the white lady glows in the dark like a flame. By her it's peaceful.

TWENTY

Old Edie. Dorothy. It is dark. There is no electricity. Candles.

Dorothy Why won't you talk to me? You can't just stop.

   Edie is silent.

What's the point of being an old person if you don't prattle on about bygone days?

   Silence.

I'll send you back.

Edie I can't stay here anyway, they've turned off the electricity

Dorothy I need you to talk to me because of my book.

Edie Book!

Dorothy What are you saying it like that for?

Edie I don't believe there is going to be a book. I think you've gone mad, Dorothy, if you want to know the truth. I think I might have been a bit hasty in my counsel about them pills. Looks like you could do with a few.

Dorothy Talk to me.

Edie No. It's not doing you any good and even an old baggage like me has the right to a bit of privacy.

Dorothy If you don't talk to me I'm going to shoot myself.

   Dorothy pulls the gun out from under a chair.

Edie Do me first.

Dorothy I'm not shooting my own aunty.

Edie But I give you permission, Dorothy.

Dorothy No, and that's final.

Edie I was happy in that home.

Dorothy You were not.

Edie Happy and vegetating, and you dragged me to this place with no modern conveniences. It's Friday tomorrow. We always had a nice bit of fish on a Friday.

Dorothy Stop playing the innocent old woman.

Edie Wake up, Dorothy. You've got something to live for. What have I got? You've got Tom.

Tom enters. He carries a box.

Tom What are you up to Dorothy?

Dorothy She's not talking to me.

Tom Haven't you got enough tales for your book?

Dorothy This isn't about a stupid book, Tom.

Tom What is it about, then?

Dorothy I like talking about old times. It's all I do like.

Tom throws down the box.

Dorothy What's that?

Tom A box.

Dorothy Take it away.

Tom No. It's mine and it's yours. I've signed papers for it.

Dorothy Take it away, Tom.

Tom I'm not staying. The car's outside. I've come to say something. About Marion.

Dorothy Marion?

Tom We know what happened to her. We've known for years.

Dorothy We don't know. Nobody knows.

Tom Yes, they do.

Dorothy Bones. That's all they had. You're not telling me that a lovely young woman can end up just like that.

Tom Yes. That is exactly what I'm saying. And you know it too only we've gone on pretending for years. I've pretended that I didn't know you were pretending. It's just twisted us up and now it's spat us out and look at us. Hopeless.

Dorothy You can't stand there and tell me that what they showed us was our daughter.

Tom Yes. I can. Come and take a look. (*He goes to open the box.*)

Dorothy Don't touch that box, Tom.

Tom I don't want to but I have to.

Dorothy (*shouts*) No no. I hate you. Leave me alone.

Tom It's as if we've buried ourselves here instead of burying her.

Dorothy (*shouts*) Get out.

Tom Dorothy.

Dorothy (*shouts*) Out. (*quietly*) Or I'll shoot.

Tom You'll have to do it this time. (*Tom opens the box. He kneels beside it.*) Marion. It's Dad. It's alright. You're home now. D's here too. They know, D, because of several things. Because of when she fractured her wrist. Because of her teeth. She's been waiting there for us to come and collect her for years and we never came.

Dorothy No. No. That's not true.

Tom That's Marion in that box. Come and look.

Dorothy No. I won't look.

Tom I've signed the papers now.

Dorothy Throw that bloody box of trash out.

Tom grabs Dorothy and makes her look in the box.

Tom Look!

Dorothy No! (*She looks. Looks away.*)

Tom Dorothy?

Dorothy Get out.

Tom I'll be outside.

He exits.
Dorothy looks back at box.

Edie Bloody bloody hell. I will tell you something, Dorothy. I lost a baby once . . .

Young Edie, Gladys and Margery enter the scene. Their reality is that of fifty years earlier. Margery gives Young Edie a cup of tea. Young Edie is in her night-gown.

Margery Tea. Hot tea. With sugar.

Gladys Did you put two in, Margery?

Margery Three.

Old Edie (*to Dorothy*) I'd make tea only there's no hot water.

Gladys Put a drop of brandy in it.

She hands Margery a brandy bottle. Margery pours some into a spoon.

Don't bother with a spoon. Tip it in. You have some an' all, Margery, and then give it to me.

Old Edie You need something stronger.

Edie takes brandy bottle and gives some to Dorothy in a tea cup. She has some too. She puts it into Dorothy's hands.

Old Edie Drink up.

Gladys (*to Young Edie*) Drink up.

They both do.

Young Edie What was it?

Gladys It was a little boy. He was lovely, wasn't he, Margery?

Margery He was.

Gladys And he was peaceful, like a little angel. He didn't suffer.

Margery It was like he was asleep, wasn't it?

Gladys I've seen them before like that. It's always the same. Just like they're sleeping. Like they never wanted to wake up. Like angels.

Dorothy She was like an angel. My angel.

Old Edie (*to Dorothy*) You cry.

Gladys (*to Young Edie*) Have a good cry.

Edie Mum and Margery sat up with me.

Gladys You fetch your christening dress, Margery.

Margery does so.

Old Edie Mum dressed him.

Gladys He'll look beautiful in that. That's hand-made lace, Edie. What do you think?

71

Young Edie Yes. I like that.

Old Edie Yes. Beautiful.

Dorothy And you stayed with him all night.

Old Edie Yes, we did.

Lights fade on tableau of all women watching the night out.

Old Edie My mother was very hard.

I never like to remember that night because she weren't hard then, she was kind, and it made me think what we could have been like if things had been different. She did know things. Perhaps it's so far off now I can see it.

Pregnant woman enters followed by Tom.

Pregnant Woman Hello? Hello? It's dark in here, isn't it? I expect that's because there's no electricity.

Tom I don't think now is a good time . . .

Pregnant Woman Look, I had absolutley no idea. About what this place meant to you. That's not the way you think when you're buying, is it? I've come to apologise, I suppose. I've been lying awake at night and John, my husband, said, 'Well why don't you go and talk to her if you feel so bad?' There's a court order you know. I mean it is only a matter of time. John was saying that you could have asked for money. From your landlord, a sort of pay off. That often makes people feel better. You would have got something back then. We know someone who got ten thousand pounds. But that was Earls Court. Still, all the same. These cost tuppence to build you know and now they're worth a pretty penny. I was wondering whether you should still try it. The money, I mean. Look, here's my mobile phone number. (*She passes her a piece of paper.*) If you want to talk to me, discuss anything. Please ring me. We really don't want any hold-ups. The baby's due in thirteen weeks. John says we could stretch to a thousand. Now I don't now what the landlord will offer but I bet you could double it. So think about it and please ring me. I'd so much prefer all this to end happily. I want the ghosts of the house to like me. (*Addresses them.*) I'm not so very bad.

Edie Do you still have that gun, Dorothy? Oh yes, there it is. (*She picks up the gun.*) Please leave the premises or we will be forced to shoot you.

Pregnant Woman I know that's a bad joke.

Tom Not necessarily.

Edie Still, we've been law-abiding this long, it's a pity to spoil it.

Pregnant Woman Oh my god. It's as bad as Birmingham. (*She exits.*)

Dorothy Tom.

Tom holds Dorothy.

It's time to leave, isn't it?

Tom I think so. We've got to get something sorted out, properly. Marion. We could do it now. I've got the forms. Leave here. Goodbye to it all.

He holds forms. Dorothy takes them.

Dorothy (*reads*) Statutory application for cremation. Form A to be signed and completed by person applying.

Tom Me or you, I suppose.

Dorothy A complete set of medical forms must be supplied. Forms B and C.

Tom That's the blue ones.

Dorothy The doctor attending the deceased fills in form B, a second independent doctor form C. The documents are scrutinised by a medical referee whom once satisfied signs form F.

Tom Yes. It's quite complicated.

Dorothy Bollocks to that, Tom.

Edie Yes. Bugger that, Tom.

Tom If you say so.

Dorothy We're going to do it ourselves.

Tom What?

Edie Bury her ourselves.

Tom Marion.

Dorothy Today. We'll make her beautiful.

Edie She can have my necklace.

Dorothy Mum's wedding ring.

Edie I've got some bright things. Bits of ribbon.

Dorothy Dad's medals.

Tom We'll say some words.

Dorothy We'll find somewhere beautiful for her.

Tom In the woods or somewhere.

Dorothy We'll find somewhere. We'll find somewhere.

They pick up box. Exit.

TWENTY-ONE

*A double bed filled with people dressed in coats. It is
winter. A storm blows outside. A large tree creaks down
and drops down on top of it. Cries. Silence. Then one by
one they call to each other and pop up through its
branches. They share the following dialogue:*

Edie? You okay? Margery? Diggie? Winnie? Ellen?
Albert? What happened? The tree crashed in through the
roof. I heard it going. Creaking then eeeeergh SMASH.
What do we do now? Wait for Mum and Dad. I heard
the pottie smash. Are we angels? Matilda Salmon saw an
angel in the churchyard once. There's Roman treasure
buried under the village cross. We dug it up once, didn't
we, but then we put it back. Once the whole village died,
dead of the plague and the wind was whistling but there
was nobody there 'cos they were DEAD! Shut up you're
scaring us! What'll happen? What'll we be when we
grow up? Our village won't be dead? Maybe we can
miss school tomorrow? You can't go to school if you've
been hit on the head by a tree. Let's hold hands and
wait. Wait for someone to come. Does anyone know a
poem or a song? We could sing that while we're waiting,
or does anyone know a story. You do, Edie. Go on.
Tell it.